A SPIRIT DAUGHTER
WORKBOOK

---

written by
Jill Wintersteen

FOR THE AQUARIUS SEASON
January 19th - February 18th

+

THE NEW MOON
Thursday, February 11th, 2021
11:05 AM PST

AQUARIUS

From the structure and order of Capricorn, we land in the open-minded and vast airwaves of Aquarius. This first Sun Season of 2021 brings us inspiration, illumination, and a glimpse of the future. Aquarius is the rebellious, freedom-loving, progressive Air sign of the zodiac. This energy helps to break society's rules and form new paradigms better suited for the evolution of humanity. Aquarius allows us to think outside of the proverbial box and process the world through our unique filter. This season is a time to dig passed the layers of societal conditioning placed upon you and feel your most authentic truth, then have the courage to live it.

Ruled by both Saturn and Uranus, Aquarius is an often misunderstood energy. At its heart, Aquarius teaches us who we are beyond what we were told to be. It is the sign of individuality and fearless self-expression. Aquarius stirs up the part of us that beats to their own drum and cares not what others think of the song. Aquarius teaches us to question everything and ask if it is our truth. We often take on other people's truths. Much of culture is passed down in this manner, where ideologies and societal norms are merely patterns we pick up on as children. We take on these collective energies as our reality until we question them. This season is a time to find the answers we seek.

The flip side of Aquarius, and the part that can become confusing, is it is also the sign of the collective. So while it teaches us to form our own truth, it also asks us to do so for the benefit of others. Aquarius teaches us that we live in a world with other people. Like all air signs, it helps us connect with others and remember that we all breathe together. What happens to one member of the collective creates a ripple effect through the planet, touching everyone's energy, whether they know it or not. While Aquarius asks us to be ourselves and break free of societal conditioning, it also asks us to respect our place in the collective and know that we contribute to a consciousness shared by all. This season helps us reconcile these two varying energies of Aquarius and merge them to help raise the vibration of the world. The key is that everyone in society lives their authentic truth from the highest frequency their energy can achieve. Part of this season's work is finding out who you are and defining your beliefs, while the other part is doing the work to raise your vibration. Ideally, we want to live in the vibration of love, compassion, peace, hope, gratitude, and joy.

Aquarius sets up lofty goals for society, but if we can all hold the vision for this type of future, it may come to fruition. Aquarius asks us to see past the current status quo and envision a new world that understands everyone's differences yet accepts everyone equally. It's a world where everyone is living their truth at their highest vibration. It may be challenging to imagine a place where everyone effectively is doing what they want, but it becomes more plausible if we add in the image of them doing what they want from love or compassion. The key to stepping into the Aquarius age is to pair knowing and living your truth while remaining in the higher energetic frequencies. We then emit these vibrations into the world, helping to elevate the collective consciousness. We also no longer absorb energies around us and can define our own truth.

As we venture through this exciting season, feel into what frequency you rest at each day. How do you feel when you wake up? What shifts you up and down the vibrational scale? For instance, if you wake up in an angry or jealous vibration, what helps you change to a state of motivation or gratitude? Conversely, if you wake up in a vibration of love, what lowers your frequency throughout the day? Our vibration can be affected by many things, some external and some internal. While the external ones we often can not control, we can control our reaction to them. Notice how your responses to the world around you changes your frequency. Also, notice how you treat yourself changes your frequency. When we do not accept and love ourselves, our vibration suffers. Aquarius teaches us to see ourselves from every angle and accept it all without judgment. Notice how self-judgment, self-doubt, and self-rejection affect you energetically. Carefully monitor your frequency and notice what you can do each day to set it at the vibrational level most beneficial for yourself and others. Know that when you do, you are raising the vibration of the world.

MOONSCOPES

The following horoscopes are based on your personal Moon Sign. Your Moon sign tells you what you need to feel emotionally fulfilled and can teach you what your heart craves. These horoscopes give guidance on how Aquarius Season and the New Moon will affect your emotions and illuminate the highest frequency of your heart.

Aries Moon: In your highest vibration, you emit the frequency of courage, motivation, and fire. Your emotions are explosive and cannot be ignored. You need to direct them to help you feel motivated instead of angry. Feel into your most fiery self this Aquarius Season and recognize your inherent power to lead. Energy like yours is not for the shadows. Step into the spotlight and speak your truth as you show others how to courageously do the same. On the New Moon, ask yourself, "How can I shift my vibration to feel my power every day?"

Taurus Moon: In your highest vibration, you emit a frequency of security, abundance, and worthiness. Your emotions are grounded in the Earth and feel centered to everyone you know. You also tend to lean towards stubbornness and get stuck in your ways. Challenge yourself this Season to shift into gratitude when you feel stagnant in your energy. Feel your natural ability to create and harness this ability to imagine a new reality, one that understands you already have everything you need. On the New Moon, ask yourself: "How can I shift into a vibration of abundance every day?"

Gemini Moon: In your highest vibration, you emit a frequency of curiosity, gratitude, and acceptance. Your emotions tend to go through many ups and downs but always bring you back to the questions which matter the most. You direct any space and relationship through the need for conversation. Throughout Aquarius Season, feel your power to change the frequency of a room through your words. Then choose words that lift the vibration of yourself and everyone around you. On the New Moon, ask yourself: "How can I include more positive vibrations while speaking my truth?"

Cancer Moon: In your highest vibration, you emit a frequency of unconditional love, compassion, and vulnerability. Your emotions run deep and can take over your energy. Challenge yourself this Season to question your perception of your feelings. Attempt to view them from different angles to understand their many layers. On the New Moon, ask yourself: "How can I still feel my emotions but not become overwhelmed by them, knowing that awareness of my feelings is what helps me shift them?"

Leo Moon: In your highest vibration, you emit a frequency of joy, open-heartedness, and leadership. You know yourself well but can struggle with expressing your truth. You naturally seek out approval in every situation even though you do not need it. Challenge yourself this Season to stand firm in your frequency, unaffected by the opinions of others. Feel into your power and know that you can change the world if you remain connected to your true self. On the New Moon, ask yourself:" How can I stand in my power in every situation even if I fear I will not be accepted?"

Virgo Moon: In your highest vibration, you emit a frequency of refinement, centeredness, and healing. You love to be of service and seek to help everyone you meet. You carry a vibration of stability that attracts more stability to you. If you remain grounded in your power, you easily shape your world to fit your visions. If you begin to look outside of yourself for validation, though, your vibration shifts, and so does what you attract. On the New Moon, ask yourself: "How can I accept myself to help raise my vibration and my ability to attract energies I need?"

Libra Moon: In your highest vibration, you emit a frequency of harmony, calmness, and patience. You love to be in partnerships and tend to merge your frequency with another quite easily. This integration makes you a wonderful partner but also can

MOONSCOPES

threaten your sense of self. Throughout Aquarius Season, begin to notice when you are not staying true to your own frequency and instead, taking on another person's vibration. On the New Moon, ask yourself: "How can I still show up for others while maintaining and emitting my own energy?"

Scorpio Moon: In your highest vibration, you emit a frequency of security, understanding, and confidence. You see the truth of every situation easily and understand it at a fundamental level. You tend to keep your truths to yourself, though, and may feel some friction this Season as Aquarius encourages you to share more of yourself with others. Throughout Aquarius Season, begin to understand that when you share your vibration with others, you shift their frequency. You help them transform. On the New Moon, ask yourself: "How can I share my truths with others in a way that raises my vibration and the vibration around me?"

Sagittarius Moon: In your highest vibration, you emit a frequency of joy, optimism, and truth. You crave freedom and seek partners who understand this about you. You carry a strong frequency and need no one to help you define it. Throughout Aquarius Season, recognize your power to change the vibration of any space. Take your ability to the next level by infusing your natural joy and positivity into every situation. Stand firm in your frequency and watch others take on your optimism. On the New Moon, ask yourself: "How can I shift into a positive vibration every day and share it with the world around me?"

Capricorn Moon: In your highest vibration, you emit a frequency of strength, resolve, and focus. You are grounded in your vibration and are not easily influenced by others. You do need space for yourself to process the world and refine your frequency. This space serves to amplify your energy and help you understand it. Throughout Aquarius Season, feel into your stability and extend it to those around you who need some grounding. Realize that your vibration can help everyone you meet and find ways to share it with the collective on a broader level. On the New Moon, ask yourself: "How can I ground my vibration even more so it becomes a positive anchor for myself and those who need it most?"

Aquarius Moon: In your highest vibration, you emit a frequency of uniqueness, innovation, and creativity. You crave the ability to invent solutions often to only problems you see. You understand the world through a different lens than most people and use this information to create your reality. Throughout this Season, fully align with Aquarius and your emotions. When the Sun is in your Moon sign, your feelings are activated at a greater level. Feel into who you are and who you want to be. Also, feel how you can shift and change your vibration to match your authentic self. On the New Moon, ask yourself: "How can my unique vibration teach and change the world?"

Pisces Moon: In your highest vibration, you emit a frequency of imagination, expansiveness, and healing. You have the power to expand your vibration to encompass any space and everyone in it. Your energy hugs people like a warm blanket, making you a great healer. You tend, though, to pick up unwanted vibrations, and this can block your creativity. Learn how to release energies just as quickly as you pick them up and feel your life take on a new rhythm. Align with this Season to teach you how to shift from one vibration to another merely through conscious attention and effort. Know that you are always connected to the collective consciousness and draw inspiration from your infinite connection to everything. On the New Moon, ask yourself: "How can I align with my creativity and use it to help me emit a frequency of compassion?"

You can look up your Moon Sign at astro-charts.com

CRYSTALS FOR AQUARIUS

Peacock Ore, or bornite, is a stone of happiness. It promotes joy by dispelling any negative energy of the space or the person wearing it. It also helps to align and activate all the chakras, bringing full integration to the energetic system. In doing so, it sheds the lower frequencies of the body and makes space for the higher ones to flourish. It is also an excellent healing stone. Try placing a piece on one area of your body and feel it align the rest of your system with its energy. Peacock Ore is vibrant in color, generally electric blue with hints of the rainbow.

Peacock Ore vibrates to the mantra: "I am happy."

Goldstone is made from quartz and sand, then infused with copper particles. Goldstone is an excellent stone for helping you visualize your goals and achieve them. Its energy enhances your imagination, increasing your powers of innovation and bringing out your inner genius. Once you have your vision firmly in place, Goldstone brings ease, grace, and magic to manifesting it. Goldstone is copper in color with shimmery flecks.

Goldstone vibrates to the mantra, "I am golden."

Kambaba Jasper is a rare type of jasper known for carrying the energy of tranquility and peace. It helps to stabilize your frequency and ground you in the present moment. It also helps to release negative emotions such as self-doubt and criticism. In doing so, it brings about courage and the willingness to leap into new situations. Kambaba Jasper will help you tap into the part of you who is fearless and ready to take action from a place of peace. It is dark green with swirls of a crocodile.

Kambaba Jasper vibrates to the mantra, "I am stable."

K2 is a powerful stone that opens up a portal to higher consciousness. It illuminates your intuition and can give you glimpses of the future. While opening up your third eye, it also keeps you grounded in your body, helping to practically apply the knowledge you gain while working with it. Hold K2 while meditating, sitting quietly with it in your left hand to receive new insight and inspiration. You can also place it on your third eye while lying down, meditating on its cool texture as you drift into a higher vibration. K2 is white with flecks of blue/green.

K2 vibrations to the mantra: "I am aware."

Moss Agate is considered a stone of abundance. It brings abundance in all forms, including the courage needed to pursue challenging goals. It brings strength and vitality to help us fight battles both with ourselves and the outside world. If you feel misunderstood, Moss Agate will give you the strength to defend your true self. It will also ease the pain of feeling misplaced without community. Have some with you if you are traveling to new communities or forming a new collective. This crystal will bring you grounding and reconnect you with Mother Earth. This connection will lessen any fear or stress of a new situation and restore balance to your entire system. Moss Agate is translucent green in color.

Moss Agate vibrates to the mantra: " I am fearless."

AQUARIUS MEDITATION

Loving Kindness, or Metta, is a Buddhist meditation that inspires compassion and unconditional love for all beings. It has been taught all over the world, and there are many different forms of this meditation. Try practicing it every morning to expand your heart frequency and become more in touch with the vibration of love and compassion. Through this practice, cultivate a love for yourself and others.

Begin in a comfortable, relaxed position. You can be lying down or in a seated position. Begin to breathe into your heart, feeling your chest expand and contract on each inhale and exhale. Imagine your heart as a circle of light and feel it growing with each breath. Begin to think of someone you love; this can be anyone in your life, even a pet. Feel the love you have in your heart for this being and see them in their happiest state. As you hold this vision of them, say, "May you be happy, may you be healthy, may you be free."

Now direct your attention back to yourself and feel your heart expanding. Imagine yourself in your happiest state and say to yourself, "May I be happy, may I be healthy, may I be free."

Return your attention to others. Envision everyone you love in their happiest state. You can go through each person one at a time, seeing them smiling and in full enjoyment of life. Say to each of them, "May you be happy, may you be healthy, may you be free."

Bring your awareness now to people who are neutral in your life. These people can be co-workers or acquaintances of some type, someone you do not have strong feelings for. Envision them in their happiest state, even if you've never seen it in reality. Say to them, "May you be happy, may you be healthy, may you be free."

Lastly, and often the hardest, bring your attention to someone who you have negative feelings towards. This person can be someone who has hurt you in the past or someone who you feel jealousy or resentment towards. Envision that person in their happiest state and say to them, "May you be happy, may you be healthy, may you be free."

Close the meditation by bringing your awareness to your heart. Radiate this feeling of love out into the universe. See the light of your heart expand passed your body, room, and even city. Say to yourself, "May all beings of this universe be happy, healthy, and free."

There are many variations of the phrases you can say; feel free to add or adjust them in any way. The main point is to send these feelings of loving-kindness to everyone in the world.

AQUARIUS LUNAR FLOW

Aquarius rules the circulatory system, the ankles, and the calves. Her Season is the time to move your body and increase blood flow to the extremities. Often arising in the cold of winter, Aquarius is the time to make sure your body can keep up with the activity this Season brings to the mind. The following sequence will get your blood flowing and bring some extra attention to your calves and ankles.

Sun Salutation A // Surya Namaskar A- 3 rounds
Stand at the top of your mat. Inhale, stretch your arms overhead. Exhale fold forward. Inhale lengthen out your back. Exhale step back to plank pose and lower. Inhale, reach your chest up for Upward Facing Dog. Exhale to Downward Dog Pose. Stay here for 5 breaths and feel your entire body expand. On Exhale, step to the top of the mat. Inhale lengthen through your spine. Exhale fold forward. Inhale come up to standing, reaching arms overhead. Exhale with hands to your heart. Pause for a moment and feel yourself centered throughout your body. Continue this for 5 rounds, feeling the rhythm of the breath and body moving together. Allow this rhythm to soothe your mind and body.

Sun Salutation B // Surya Namaskar B- 3 rounds
Stand at the top of your mat. Inhale, stretch your arms overhead and bend your knees into Chair Pose > Exhale, fold forward > Inhale, lengthen out your back > Exhale, step into plank pose and lower halfway to Chatarunga (elbows into ribs) > Inhale, reach your chest up for Upward-Facing Dog, with everything off the ground except your hands and feet > Exhale, Downward Dog Pose > Inhale, step left foot forward to Warrior 1, with the back foot flat at a 45 degree angle, bend into the front knee and lift your arms to the sky, 5 breaths here > Exhale, release into plank > lower to Chatarunga > Inhale into Upward Facing Dog > Exhale, Downward Facing Dog. Repeat on right side, then remain in Downward Dog for 5 breaths > Exhale, step to the top of the mat > Inhale, lengthen through your spine > Exhale, fold forward > Inhale, Chair Pose > Exhale, hands to heart, breathe at the top of your mat as you feel your energy circulating throughout your body.

Lunge > Twisted Lunge > Ardha Hanumanasana
From standing, step your right foot back into Lunge pose, bending the front knee to a 90-degree angle. Inhale, reach your arms overhead, spreading your fingers wide. Take five breaths here. On exhale, reach your right arm forward, left arm back, twisting to the left. Reach through both arms as you draw your lower belly in and breathe into your lungs for 5 breaths. On exhale, release the twist and lower the hands to either side of the front foot. Lower the back knee down and straighten through the front leg for half splits pose. Flex the front foot as you reach the chest towards the toes. Breath deeply for 5 breaths, lengthening out the back of the leg. On exhale, re-bend the front knee, step back to plank pose. Either go through a vinyasa, or go straight back to downward dog. Repeat on the second side. End back at the top of the mat.

AQUARIUS LUNAR FLOW

Warrior 1 > Parsvottansana > Twisted Triangle

Step your right foot back into Warrior 1. Place your back foot flat at a 45-degree angle and bend into your front knee. Inhale, lift your arms overhead for 5 breaths. Exhale, lower your arms, placing your hands on your waist. Hop the back foot in about 12 inches and straighten the front leg for parsvottanasana. Keep the back foot angled in at 45 degrees. Inhale, extend through the chest, exhale, fold forward over the leg. Keep your hands at your waist, and extend through the chest, keeping the back flat. Spend 5 breaths here, then inhale up to standing. Inhale, reach the right arm to the sky, lengthening the right waist. Exhale, fold forward placing the right hand to the inside of the left foot on, or off, a block. Rotate your spine to the left, as you reach your left arm to the sky. Lengthen through the spine as you twist deeper on each exhale. Spend 5 breaths here, then release both hands to either side of the front foot. Step back into plank, going through a vinyasa or straight to downward dog. Repeat on the other side, ending back at the top of the mat.

Twisted Chair

Return to the front of your mat. Keep your feet together and bend deeply into your knees as if you were sitting in a chair. Reach your arms upward to the sky and look up. Feel your belly drawing in, helping to direct your tailbone to the floor. Bring your hands to heart center, palms pressing. On Exhale twist to the left, hook your right elbow on the outside of your left knee for leverage. Hips stay square as you twist deeper on each exhale. Feel your two sides integrating as you twist across your spine. Take 5 breaths in the twist, then return to center, forward fold over your legs for a breath. Return to chair pose and repeat the twist on the right side for 5 breaths then fold forward once again. Allow your spine and neck to fully release in this fold, holding it for 5 breaths. You may grab ahold of opposite elbows and bend your knees slightly if needed. Once you are finished, place your hands on your hips and Inhale to standing.

Standing Forward Bend

Straighten your legs, still standing at the top of your mat. Inhale, reach your arms up to the sky, exhale, fold forward into a Standing Forward Bend. Slightly bend your knees and allow your whole spine to release. You may clasp either elbow or release your hands to the ground. Fill your lungs up with air on each breath as your neck, head, and shoulders relax. Spend 10 breaths here, feeling your entire nervous system slow down. Once finished, return to standing.

Eagle Pose // Garudasana

Standing at the top of the mat, slightly bend the knees. Slowly, pick up the right leg wrapping it around the left for Eagle Pose. First cross thigh over thigh, like you were sitting in a chair, then try to tuck your right foot behind left calf. Stretch your arms straight forward, parallel to the floor. Cross your left arm over the right, bending your elbows. Cross once at the upper arms and a second time with the hands if possible. Raise your forearms perpendicular to the ground and reach them away from you, spreading the back. Stare at one point to maintain your balance. Take 5 deep breaths here, then release. Repeat on the other side.

Child's Pose

From the top of your mat, lower to the ground for child's pose. Reach your arms out in front of you and feel your forehead resting on the ground, connecting with the Earth's energy and stillness. Take 5 breaths, then extend your arms and torso to the right, still in Child's Pose. Take 5 breaths, breathing into the left side ribs. Come back to center and switch sides.

Savasana: 5 minutes

Stretch your legs out long on the mat. Have your palms facing upward in a receptive motion. Allow your entire weight to be supported by the floor beneath you as you rest. Let go of counting the breath and just breathe naturally, observing the quiet flow of inhale and exhale.

ALIGNING the SPIRIT

Tips for Aligning your Authentic Truth

"she lives in a world of her own imagination, where reality is what she makes it and the only thing holding her back is herself.

fueled by stardust and a vision of the future,
she leaves a trail of magic as she dances to her own rhythm never stopping to conform to anyone's expectations but her own."

- spirit daughter

As humans, we crave the ability to express ourselves authentically. We also desire to see this skill in our leaders, guides, and mentors. When we meet someone who feels real to us, we automatically trust them, listen to them, and want to embody their same confidence. Our deepest desire is to be ourselves in every situation. This authenticity requires we have the freedom to do so and the confidence to allow ourselves to be vulnerable, seen, and even judged. Aligning with, and being, our authentic truth is a journey - the that Aquarius Season can help us travel. Below are some tips on how to feel your most authentic self this Season and always.

Know Yourself - and Be Honest:
One of the first steps to being authentic is to know yourself. This self-reflection requires you to take an honest look at who you are and the truths you hold. It's about understanding what your energy resonates with on a soul level. To find these answers, we often need to sift through layers of conditioning placed upon us. Throughout Aquarius Season, ask yourself what is true to you. What do you believe in? You, not your best friend or your partner, but what are your beliefs? What are the stories that define you, and are they aligned with your soul? Are there pieces of yourself you'd rather not look at, and how can you meet them with compassion? Get to know yourself more deeply this Season. Start each day writing down the statement "I am" and allow the rest of the sentence to flow freely from your pen. Create as many statements as you'd like each day as you unravel each layer. Challenge yourself to look at every angle of your personality- even the bits you'd rather avoid. Get to the bottom of who you really are, even if it feels vulnerable. Building awareness is always better than turning the other way. Release self-judgment and if there are things you'd like to change about yourself, take steps to do that. You can always shift your energy, but you need to understand it first. As you learn more about yourself, it will become easier to be the real you everywhere in your life.

Stop Apologizing for Being You
As you begin to step into your authenticity and speak your truth, it's natural to apologize immediately. It's usually a nervous tick that, once you become aware of, will fade. For some reason, we think our truth is offensive to others. If we speak from love and compassion, however, it is never offensive. It's important to notice if you are apologizing for being you. Catch every unneeded "I'm sorry" as it directly undermines your words. There is no need to be sorry for speaking your truth from a place of love.

ALIGNING the SPIRIT

Accept You May Be Alone:
It's ok if you are the only one who sees things in a certain way- that does not mean it's wrong. It just means you have a different perspective. We often hide our authentic truth when it doesn't match what the world around us believes. We downplay our visions and may even withhold them from others. When we live from an authentic place, we often break rules that needed to be challenged in the first place. Many great visionaries went against the status quo, and because they did, they changed life for all of us. When you align with your authenticity, you blaze a new trail. Over this Season, notice if you are holding back out of fear of being the only one who believes a certain truth. Ask yourself if that truth is what you genuinely believe and if it is, share it with others. Stand up for what you believe, even if you're the only one standing. If others resonate with your visions, you won't be standing alone for long.

Be You in Every Arena:
Allow your authenticity to infuse everything you do. We tend to hold our real selves out of certain areas of our life. Perhaps we hide pieces of personality from certain friends or co-workers or don't speak our truth to our parents. It's natural to want to people-please and impress others who are important to you, but not at the expense of your truth. Being you may ruffle some feathers and may even cause others to look at you differently, but that's ok. We weren't put on this Earth to please everyone. We were placed here to be ourselves and align with our soul's mission. To honor the energy we hold, we need to be our most authentic self in every area, even if we are not liked. It's more important that you like yourself, and that comes from living your truth.

Trust Yourself and Your Intuition:
This step is one of the most important points on this list; you must trust yourself. If it's true to you- it's true. If you feel it, it's real. Even if other's try to invalidate your experience, know that your reality is enough. Use meditation to center yourself and journal to clarify your thoughts and feelings. Also, learn to listen to your intuition. It is always guiding you and is in touch with your most authentic self.

Embrace Vulnerability:
Vulnerability is necessary for living an authentic life. Yes, it is scary. Yes, it feels uncomfortable, but it is part of the process. Know that vulnerability is experienced by everyone who is speaking and standing in their truth. It's often a clue that you are on the right track and bearing your true self to the world. The greatest leaders of our time feel vulnerable too. That's what makes them great leaders- they feel the fear of vulnerability but stand in their truth despite it.

Ask for Support:
It's not always easy to speak your truth, especially if you are trying to incite change. Ask the closest people to you to listen or review your work. As you open up to trusted sources, it will be easier to speak your truths to others.

Love (and celebrate) Yourself:
Knowing ourselves is one thing, loving ourselves is another. When we truly love who we are, we more easily show our true self to others. We step into our authenticity with confidence, knowing that we will always love ourselves no matter what the world thinks about us. We also release self-judgment more easily. We have compassion for our journey and know that every up and down is part of the process that makes us who we are. It's also important to celebrate ourselves. This involves appreciating your unique personality. Throughout Aquarius Season, make a list of things you love and appreciate about yourself. What are you celebrating about yourself each day? As you look over this list, allow it to help you be your most authentic self to yourself and to the world. When you genuinely love yourself, you can't help but be you.

NEW MOON

FEBRUARY 11TH

AQUARIUS IN THE:	FOCUS ON...
1ST HOUSE	Focus on shifting your frequency around your identity and how you project yourself to the world.
2ND HOUSE	Focus on shifting your frequency around how you view wealth, resources, and your ability to create abundance.
3RD HOUSE	Focus on shifting your frequency around how you communicate with yourself and others.
4TH HOUSE	Focus on shifting your frequency around how you feel about self-care and how you receive support from others.
5TH HOUSE	Focus on shifting your frequency around how you view play and incorporating more joy into your life.
6TH HOUSE	Focus on shifting your frequency around how you view service and how you give your gifts to the world.
7TH HOUSE	Focus on shifting your frequency around how you exchange energy in relationships and how you merge vibrations with partners.
8TH HOUSE	Focus on shifting your frequency around your personal growth and how you view your shadow side.
9TH HOUSE	Focus on shifting your frequency around expanding your horizons and how you integrate new information.
10TH HOUSE	Focus on shifting your frequency around your life's work and how you find fulfillment in pursuing it.
11TH HOUSE	Focus on shifting your frequency around how you raise the vibration of the collective.
12TH HOUSE	Focus on shifting your frequency around your spiritual health and your path to enlightenment.

NEW MOON

FEBRUARY 11TH

Each month, the Moon makes her way around the Earth, shifting the Sun's illumination on her as she dances through our sky. We feel her rhythm of waxing and waning until she returns to the New Moon phase and the start of a new Lunar Cycle. This return to darkness also marks her monthly meeting with the Sun. During a New Moon, the Sun and the Moon are together in the sky. This conjunction is one of the most powerful aspects in astrology. The combination of these energies and the combined gravitational pull they exhibit makes the New Moon a potent time to harness the cosmos' energy to create and design our lives.

On a New Moon, the combined effect of both Sun and Moon create a subtle frequency that is felt in our consciousness. Consciousness, in its simplest definition, is an awareness of external stimuli. One theory is that consciousness takes place at the point where differing energies intersect. It extends far passed our physical bodies and grants us the ability to perceive things we cannot see. It also allows us to be affected by subtle energies, such as the Moon. When we work with the Moon's energy, we build awareness around these shifts in consciousness and direct them to how we see fit.

Our consciousness consists of varying levels. Some are at the forefront of our awareness and are easy to work with, while others are buried deep below the psyche's surface in our subconscious. Our subconscious contains conditioned patterns from childhood, hidden fears, hidden dreams, and our true authentic self. It is a myriad of energies that direct us without our awareness. During a New Moon, the additional frequencies provided by the Sun and Moon conjunction help bring our subconscious energies to the surface of our mind so we may see and work with them. The New Moon reveals our deepest truths, what we truly desire, and all of the internal blocks that prevent us from attracting the life of our dreams.

With our deepest energies available to work with, the New Moon becomes a time to find out who we really are, what patterns inform our behavior, and what raw emotions are buried beneath our logical mind. It's also a time to access our intuition and our higher knowing. Our inner guidance exists in both our conscious and subconscious minds, ready to direct our path. Often, this knowledge is buried beneath hidden emotions, waiting for us to listen. On the New Moon, our intuition is heightened, and we have a deeper access to the part of us that knows the answers to the questions we seek. It also reveals the questions we need to ask ourselves to form a vision of the path we need to take to manifest the dreams that resonate with our authentic self.

The combined energy of the Sun and Moon are affected, or flavored, by the zodiac sign in which they are positioned. A New Moon is always in the same sign as the current Sun sign, making the qualities of this zodiac more prevalent in our lives, our minds, and our energy. Each month we can theme the work we do leading up to and on the New Moon with the aspects of the zodiac sign. These energies are swirling all around us. Why not use them to create your best life?

We can further focus our vibration based on what house this New Moon is transiting in our natal chart. You can look up your natal chart at astro-charts.com and locate the house governed by Aquarius for you. Houses represent arenas in our life. They tell us where to expect astrological energies to show up. We all have a house touched by Aquarius in our chart. It may be a piece of a house, or it may even be two houses, but we all have an Aquarius house. Find yours and then focus your intentions towards this area of your life to go further in harness the power of this New Moon.

AQUARIUS X THE NEW MOON

This second New Moon of 2021 is supercharged by the energy of Aquarius. We have the Moon and Sun in Aquarius, joined by Venus, Mercury, Saturn, and Jupiter. The Water Bearer's energy is at maximum strength, with six cosmic bodies landing in this Air sign bringing us plenty of inspiration, innovation, and clarity to inform our intentions. This New Moon's main message teaches us that our thoughts, emotions, and actions make up our energetic field and influence the frequency we emit from that field. The vibration we put out into the world attracts the vibrations we receive and our ability to manifest our visions. It also contributes to the collective frequency, helping to shape it.

This New Moon is a strong reminder that it's time to stop absorbing frequencies around you and instead define them. It's also a reminder to do the work needed to vibrate at your highest potential. When we vibrate at our highest frequency from a place of authenticity, we become unstoppable, and the world changes for the better because of our presence. As you write your intentions feel into the frequency they need from you to manifest. What vibration do you need to emanate into the world to attract your dreams? What work do you need to do each day to reach that vibrational level that matches your authentic self? On this New Moon, commit to shifting your frequency each day. Begin by taking steps to know yourself at your deepest level, including your beliefs, what makes your heart smile, what you are willing to fight for, and what you want to contribute to the collective. Take your time in learning who you are. You may not uncover every layer on this New Moon but create a routine that will help you discover your authentic truth. Then decide the vibration you want to live at throughout each day. Create practices that help you reach this energy and remain there.

Adjusting your frequency not only helps you; it helps the collective. Aquarius reminds us that we all live in an interconnected web of energy encompassing every being on the planet. What affects you also affects your neighbor even when you don't realize it. We each emanate a ripple that affects the overall current, that is the vibration of the world. We are an intricate piece of the grand puzzle of life, and every energy on this planet is needed at this time. This concept of interconnectedness is why Aquarius has become the sign synonymous with equality for all peoples. If we are truly connected to everyone else, then we understand what's good for us is good for others, and vice versa. We naturally want all people to be treated fairly and have the same opportunities because we are also affected by their life path. We are one vibration made up of individuals, merely an extension of one another.

Aquarius goes even further to teach us that what we think, feel, and speak contributes to the collective consciousness. If we are all interconnected through our vibrational frequency, then so is our consciousness. Our shared consciousness makes it essential to become aware of when we enter lower vibratory emotional states like fear or anger. These frequencies not only affect us but feed into the collective consciousness. This is why it is said that fear is contagious. When we feel fear, we send out that vibration into the world and influence people we don't even know. When we step back from society, we can see how vibrations like fear, scarcity, and anger ripple through the collective, spreading from person to person. In dealing with these vibrations, it becomes imperative that you feel your truth. Are you really scared? or angry? Do you really believe there is not enough? Or are you merely pulling in the collective energy into your consciousness? If your truth doesn't resonate with vibrations you are experiencing, shift your frequency, and work on emitting that energy into the world instead of absorbing the collective consciousness. In doing this, you'll raise the collective's vibration and help others who have not yet learned to define their own frequency. Aquarius is all about elevating the world's vibration. On this New Moon, unravel how you can help with this mission through your own magic and frequency.

AQUARIUS X THE NEW MOON

Let's look at the other planets in Aquarius, contributing to the power of this New Moon. The Sun and the Moon land at 23° Aquarius, the closet planet to them is Mercury at 16°. Mercury is currently retrograde. Mercury Retrograde is nothing to fear, and you do not want to contribute more fear into the collective energy. Mercury Retrograde can help us go inward and hear ourselves more clearly. It can provide clarity to our intentions and teach us what we truly want in this life. It can also show us how we are speaking through our frequency this New Moon. Allow Mercury Retrograde to teach you the language of your energy. What does your vibration say before you can even speak? Our energy arrives moments before our physical body. What does your frequency tell others who are awaiting your arrival? What subtle ways does your vibration communicate, and how do you want it to communicate?

Next up, we have Venus and Jupiter landing together at 12° Aquarius. Venus helps us connect to what we love and find beautiful in the world. Align with Venus's energy to return to love when you have shifted away from it. What helps you feel love in your heart and emit love to the world? Venus is expanded by Jupiter, who is the planet of faith and luck. Jupiter reminds us of our highest potential in this world. It lures us up the proverbial mountaintop by reminding us of how satisfied we will feel once we reach the pinnacle. The pairing of Jupiter and Venus this New Moon is a perfect match. Love is one of the highest vibrations we can reach as humans. It is our fullest potential. When we emit love, we raise the vibration of everyone around us. Reaching, and remaining, in a state of love is much like climbing a mountain. There are many things in the world which lower our vibration. It takes commitment and focus to remain in the frequency of love. Jupiter and Venus remind us, this New Moon, that the effort is worth it.

Saturn lands at 6° Aquarius, this New Moon, forming a square aspect with Uranus, who lands at 7° Taurus. These two planets will form an exact square (90°) on February 17th, one of three exact squares this year. Saturn in Aquarius reminds us of our personal responsibility to the collective. It teaches us that the energy we attract and emit affects everyone around us. It also brings in the element of karma, reminding us that what we do and say has consequences. If we vibrate at a higher level, then the consequences of our actions are always beneficial for ourselves and others. Saturn encourages us to commit to higher frequencies and know that they are our responsibility to create.

The square of Saturn and Uranus brings in an interesting energy this New Moon, as both are rulers of Aquarius. Saturn is the traditional ruler, guiding society's rules, and Uranus is the modern ruler, breaking them. Squares tend to crack open energies and rearrange them. Saturn and Uranus squaring creates cracks in systems governing us, including our own energy. This square so close to the New Moon brings the opportunity to shake off energies that have been controlling you. It's a time to challenge the rules you have set for yourself and recommit your energy to what resonates with your soul. Are there any commitments to the past you need to free yourself from to form a new vision of your future?

As you work with the abundance of Aquarian energies this New Moon, feel into your future self. Who are you becoming? Imagine a version of you that has broken free of the conditioned layers placed upon them and confidently lives their authentic truth. Who is this person? What do you want to feel each day, and what vibration do you want to carry? Feel how you affect everyone around you with your frequency, and notice what you attract when you vibrate at different levels. What frequency is aligned with your truth and with the life you want to create? Feel your ability to raise your vibration and raise the vibration of the world.

SETTING UP for MAGIC

Each zodiac sign carries an inherent energy. With this energy comes colors, shapes, scents, and elements which match its vibration. For every New Moon, we want to incorporate as many of these frequencies as possible. While none of them are required to align with the New Moon's energy, they do help reflect the energy. Think of it as placing energetic mirrors around the room that help amplify and direct the energy. Use your intuition to guide the choice and placement of objects. Resist the urge to overthink where they belong. Let the crystals, in particular, choose their location; all you need to do is listen.

Pick a space that feels centered and stable, either inside or outside. Imagine a white light creating the circle's boundary and place candles, crystals, and other items within this boundary. Place a crystal, candle, or another piece of magic in the center to give structure to the circle. This is also where you can set up a crystal grid to help direct the energy further. For an air sign, like Aquarius, create a circular crystal grid comprised of a large spiral and a sphere in the middle. Know that your attention and awareness of the energy available is the most important thing for working with it. You can practice the exercises in this workbook in any way you choose; you can practice alone or in a group of people around a bonfire. Your willingness to open up, to look within, and expand your consciousness is the most essential piece to this day. The other pieces for calling in and aligning with the energy of Aquarius are listed below. You can combine them in any way you like.

Colors: Electric Blue, Neon colors · Shapes: Starburst | Texture/Fabric Glass
Scents: Neroli, Ylang Ylang, Spearmint, Patchouli · Flowers: Orchid, Bird of Paradise

Incorporate all four elements into your circle. Use candles for fire, a room diffuser or spray for air, crystals and flowers to represent earth, and have some water in a metal bowl or a flower vase. Once you set up your circle, cleanse the space with a smudge stick or cleansing spay, starting with the easterly corner and working clockwise around the circle. After the circle is cleansed, smudge yourself and your friends, circling your entire body top to bottom before entering the circle. Once you enter the circle envision the frequency you want to hold the circle. Do you want the circle itself to vibrate in the energy of love? Abundance? Gratitude? or maybe all of the above. Set the frequency by having everyone feel this vibration and imagine it radiating out of you, encasing the circle's perimeter. Return to this energy anytime you feel yourself become ungrounded through the practice or in need of direction. Allow it to guide your energy through this New Moon process.

You can begin the New Moon ritual by acknowledging everyone in the room. You can then continue to the yoga, if you are practicing, and then the meditation. Once you feel the room is centered, begin to talk about the astrology of the night and what it means for each of you. If it is a larger circle, you may want to designate a talking stick or crystal to give to each guest while they speak. After you've shared your understandings, continue with the questions in the workbook and the journaling portion. After everyone has finished, talk again about your experiences with the energy and the revelations which may have occurred. You can share as little or as much as you like with the group. Never feel obligated to speak; sometimes energies need time to develop before they are brought to the light of day. At this point, you may also pull some cards to help tune further into your intuitive guidance. You can use tarot cards, Goddess cards, animal medicine cards, or any other decks that may be in your toolkit.

Once you've finished the circle, close it by having everyone close their eyes, and meditate on what they are grateful for tonight and every night. You can even practice being grateful for things that haven't come your way yet. Gratitude will attract them to your energy and let the universe know you are ready to receive them. Enjoy this time to be with yourself, your heart, and your soul. Get to know yourself on a deeper level and allow your life to unfold another layer with this New Moon.

20

Lessons from Aquarius:

- you attract what you put out

- change your perspective and your reality changes

- you are the answer

- freedom exists outside of other people's opinions

- spirit daughter

NEW MOON QUESTIONS

These questions are designed to help you become clear in your intentions. Take a few deep breaths to ground yourself before answering them. Sit with each question for a moment and allow the answer to naturally arise, being open to the person you are becoming. As you write, know you are opening the door to your intuition and giving permission to your highest visions to come out and be seen.

1. What helps you feel your authentic truth? What allows you to know yourself on the deepest level?

_____

_____

_____

_____

_____

_____

_____

_____

_____

_____

_____

_____

_____

_____

_____

_____

_____

_____

_____

_____

_____

2. How does it feel to live authentically? Do you feel vulnerable? Excited? Courageous? Or any other emotion?

3. What frequency do you want to experience each day and emit into the world? What brings you into this frequency?

_____

_____

_____

_____

_____

_____

_____

_____

_____

_____

_____

_____

_____

_____

_____

_____

_____

_____

_____

_____

_____

_____

_____

_____

_____

_____

4. Envision your future self. What guidance would they give to
   the person you are today?

INTENTION SETTING

Now is the time to dream. Intention setting is about creating the vision of your best life and creating the frequency you are going to hold to manifest this life. Intentions are not goals or to-do lists; rather, they are a way of life. They shift the energy you carry with you at all times and remind you of how you want to live. They are more about energy and less about the to-do list.

As you write your intentions, remember you are creating a frequency. These are visions you intend to hold. They are not mandatory, and they can change as many times as you need them to. Do, though, attempt to create intentions that you are willing to commit to for a period of time. This can be a lunar cycle, six months until the Full Moon in Aquarius, or several years. Dedicating your energy to an intention allows you to call in what you need to manifest it more easily.

Before you write, clear your mind of any expectations of what you think you want and be open to visions appearing from your intuition. Receive guidance from yourself and the Universe. Often, we create intentions from a place of logic. We can overthink our intentions in an effort to make them concise and clear. Attempt to let your logical mind rest. Practice the yoga and the meditation sections before writing your intentions to calm your energy and open the doorway for your inner knowledge.

Once you feel settled in your mind and connected in your body, create a scene in your mind. In this scene, see your future life. Envision every detail of a day or a period of time in this life. Also, embody the feeling this life gives you. What does it feel like to live your dreams? Who is there with you? What elements are present that add detail to your intentions? Most importantly, what vibration are you feeling and emitting? What is the frequency of your dream?

After you've written your intentions, feel the energy they create in your body. Return to this energy every day throughout the lunar cycle. Remember what your visions feel like, and hold space for them to unfold in your life. After you have given yourself plenty of time to work with your vision, feel gratitude for having already received your dream. Know that it is already here, working its way into your consciousness and into your reality.

_____

_____

_____

_____

_____

_____

_____

_____

INTENTION SETTING

NEW MOON AFFIRMATIONS

Look back at the intentions and dreams you just set. Begin to notice any subtle resistance to them in your body, mind, or energy. What does that little voice inside of you say in protest to the reality you are creating. Is there any part of you that does not believe it is possible? First, make a list of any doubts, fears, or what if's that pop into your mind when reviewing your dreams. Next, make a list of statements that oppose those negative mantras. They can be the direct opposite in meaning, or they can redirect your mind to something more positive, which proves the original statement false. Create as many affirmations as you like, which support you in holding the frequency of your dream. Repeat them at the start of each day to set your vibration and help you hold your vision.

Write your old affirmations.   Write your new affirmations.

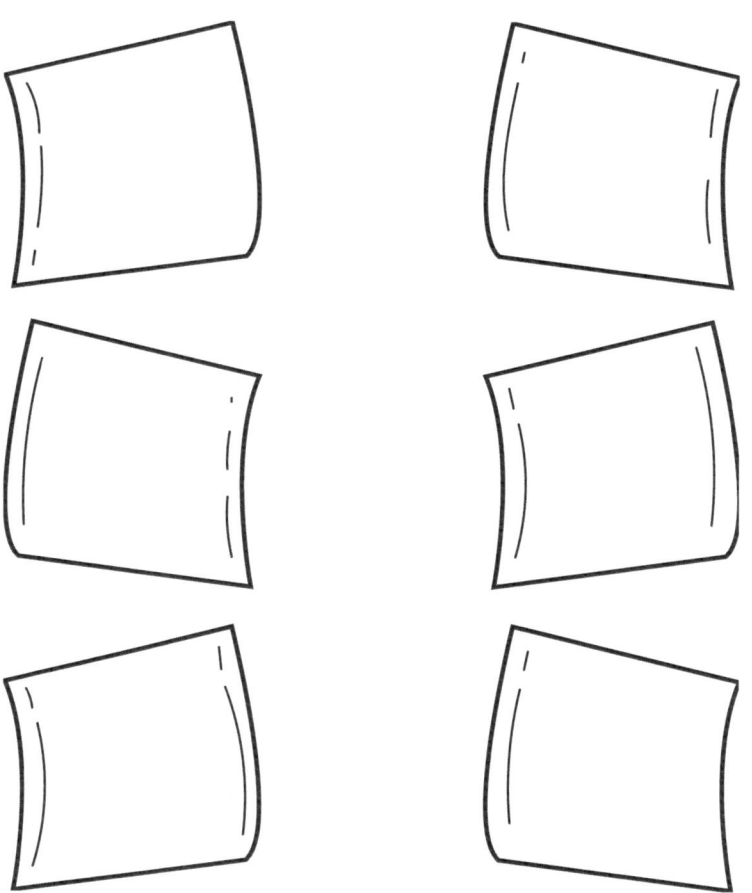

PERSONAL SIGNS

People with their Sun in Aquarius love their freedom. They are often eccentric, but can also be shy until they step into their true power. They know who they are, and they love to express themselves to the world through many different forms of media and even politics. They can often struggle in relationships as they carry many progressive views of tradition and what is supposed to occur. Their timelines often differ from others, and they never feel the need to adhere to the norm.

Aquarius Suns need to always stay true to themselves. They must learn how to stand up for what they believe, even if it goes against what others may tell them. They can be quite powerful agents of change as long as they don't fall prey to other people's assumptions or expectations. When the world tries to mold them and ask them to conform, they need to rely on themselves and have the courage to shape the world to fit their needs.

Aquarius Suns also need outlets for their creativity and unique expression. They have many ideas and need ways to share them with others. They do not require approval for their ideas; they just need to express them with the world, whether the world agrees with them or not. It is the process of expression which makes them feel fulfilled.

If Aquarius Suns do not have a creative outlet for their vast imagination and unique way of viewing the world, they can become aloof. They retreat from others and withdraw their energy from the collective, who then suffers without their energy. When they do align with this lower vibration of Aquarius, it is important they find ways to reintegrate back into the world and offer themselves in some way to humanity. They need to become involved with the collective energy to align with their highest vibration, which is leadership through innovation.

People with their Moon in Aquarius crave emotional freedom. They do quite well in relationships if they are given the freedom to be themselves. This includes the ability to process and express their emotions in a unique way. They often hold visions of partnerships that step away from the normal expectations and assumptions. They need partners who understand their uniqueness and are willing to experiment with them.

Aquarius Moons can also be shy and detached from the world. They often don't feel like they fit in with those around them, because often they don't. They have a progressive view of the world and emotions. Aquarius Moons often do not understand the common emotions which plague the rest of us, like jealousy, guilt, and fear. They live in an emotional landscape of their own making. This can make it difficult for them to relate with others and form lasting relationships. When they do, though, they often redefine the very construct in the meaning of relationship.

ASTROLOGY FORECAST

JANUARY 20TH - FEBRUARY 17TH

Jan 20th: First Quarter Moon in Taurus

The Moon in Taurus grounds our energy but also illuminates our comfort zones and attachments. The squaring of the Sun and Moon (they're 90 degrees apart) can cause tension in our emotional body. With the Sun in Aquarius still inspiring us to shift into a new vibration, the friction is between your new self and your old self, the one you are out of habit. Notice today if triggers arise, which bring out your habitual responses. Think of them as flashlights from the universe showing you the patterns you run back to simply because they are comfortable. Breakthrough this first quarter energy by changing your awareness and choose a new response and a new frequency. It will feel unfamiliar, uncomfortable, and even scary, but know these feelings are a sign of growth.

Jan 20th: Mars Conjunct Uranus in Taurus Square Jupiter and Saturn in Aquarius

Mars meets Uranus in Taurus today, adding fire to the energy of change. As the collective vibration shifts today, feel if its direction motivates you or makes you feel frustrated? How can you use the rather explosive energy of the day to make changes in your life while still feeling grounded? What actions do you want to initiate in yourself that help break up outdated patterns and open a pathway to new growth?

Jan 28th: Full Moon in Leo

Please refer to the Full Moon in Leo Workbook.

Jan 30th: Mercury Retrograde in Aquarius

Our first Mercury Retrograde of 2021 takes place in Aquarius. Mercury Retrograde is nothing to fear. It is simply a time to slow down, take deep breaths, and recalibrate your energy. Yes, it may cause some technical issues due to its governance of systems and information exchange, but we can all use a break from technology from time to time. If some device in your world breaks down, use it as an opportunity to align with nature and restore yourself.

ASTROLOGY FORECAST

JANUARY 20TH - FEBRUARY 17TH

In Aquarius, Mercury Retrograde can cause some confusion, especially when you are trying to clarify your thoughts. Be aware of contracts at this time. It's ok to sign them, but read them repeatedly and make sure you understand every detail. If you communicate with others, especially partners, know that your energy is speaking volumes even if your words don't match it. Take a step back from your interaction and center yourself. Listen to the words you are speaking and ensure they match the frequency you want to emit. It's always ok to admit you've made a mistake or misspoken. Become ok with admitting you need to rethink something or need more time to become clear. Clarify your intentions to others and allow your truth to be heard. If it doesn't feel true to you, it won't feel true to others. Allow Mercury Retrograde to help you feel into your authentic self over this transit. Get to know yourself at a deeper level and have a conversation with your soul to define your frequency.

Feb 1st: Venus enters Aquarius

Love your friends and friend your lovers. Venus, the divine feminine planet of love and beauty, enters the stars of Aquarius today. Venus brings us to the heart of the matter and helps us connect to what we love. In Aquarius, she reminds us of the joy of community and encourages us to form sisterhoods with like-minded people. Venus is Aquarius encourages us to connect with others and hear their perspectives while staying in touch with our heart and the frequency of love. Throughout this transit, feel into what helps you vibrate in the state of love, including the people who help you get there.

Feb 4th: Last Quarter Moon in Scorpio

Last Quarter Moon represents the final stage of the lunar cycle. It is the time to completely shift the energies you don't want to carry into the New Moon. Scorpio is the fearless magician of the zodiac. She is guided by her intuition alone as she traverses the unknown. She bravely dives into the depths of her own subconscious to discover the truth of her own existence. Align with the Moon and Scorpio today to take the energies and emotions, which weigh you down and turn them into something which helps you reach new heights. Take your anger or frustration, and turn it into motivation. Shift your anxiety into excitement. Find creativity and beauty amongst your sadness and depression. And, if you feel brave enough, perform the greatest alchemy and turn your deepest fears into trust. Scorpio reminds us this Moon that we create our reality, and we can create any frequency we want to live amongst. It just takes a little magic.

Feb 17th: Saturn Square Uranus Exact (first of three)

Saturn and Uranus square three times in 2021; Feb 17th, Jun 14th, and Dec 24th. Saturn rules of systems of government, our responsibilities, our commitments, and the energy of karma. Uranus is the planet that shakes things up. It governs our innovation, imagination, and ability to re-envision the future differently from today's reality. When Saturn and Uranus square, we feel friction between old commitments and new visions. It creates a crack in the system of ourselves and the systems around us. This square breaks away the outdated patterns that we once held onto for fear of losing our foundation and opens the pathway for us to form a new foundation, one strong enough to endure massive shifts in energy. As we continue to transform personally and collectively, these squares help usher in new vibrations that free us from paradigms that lower our vibration and allow for the freedom to form new ones.

✦ UP NEXT: ✦
PISCES SEASON
FEBRUARY 18TH

IT'S TIME TO DIVE INTO WHAT LIES BENEATH AND BEYOND

ENTER THE GATEWAY INTO YOUR INTUITION TO HEAL AND EXPAND
WITH THE PISCES SEASON WORKBOOK

AVAILABLE NOW!

HAPPY NEW MOON!

Thank you to everyone who supported and purchased this workbook.

Special Thanks to Rebecca Reitz (rebeccareitz.com, @becca_reitz) for her beautiful artwork on the cover, page 2, 8, 28, 30.

For a monthly subscription contact hello@spiritdaughter.com or visit www.spiritdaughter.com. Follow along our journey IG: @spiritdaughter Disclaimer: The exercises and yoga sequences in this book are physical activities that should be performed carefully to avoid injury. You agree to accept all risks and release Spirit Daughter and any guest instructors from any and all liabilities. Please take care and enjoy.